AF269672

YELLOWSTONE

Robin Koontz

Rourke
Educational Media

rourkeeducationalmedia.com

Before, During, and After Reading Activities

Before Reading: Building Background Knowledge and Academic Vocabulary

"Before Reading" strategies activate prior knowledge and set a purpose for reading. Before reading a book, it is important to tap into what your child or students already know about the topic. This will help them develop their vocabulary and increase their reading comprehension.

Questions and activities to build background knowledge:
1. *Look at the cover of the book. What will this book be about?*
2. *What do you already know about the topic?*
3. *Let's study the Table of Contents. What will you learn about in the book's chapters?*
4. *What would you like to learn about this topic? Do you think you might learn about it from this book? Why or why not?*

Building Academic Vocabulary

Building academic vocabulary is critical to understanding subject content.
Assist your child or students to gain meaning of the following vocabulary words.
Content Area Vocabulary
Read the list. What do these words mean?

- *calderas*
- *fissure*
- *fumaroles*
- *genetic*
- *historic*
- *mortality*
- *petrified*
- *refuge*
- *reservoir*
- *restoration*
- *seismographs*
- *thermophilic*

During Reading: Writing Component

"During Reading" strategies help to make connections, monitor understanding, generate questions, and stay focused.
1. *While reading, write in your reading journal any questions you have or anything you do not understand.*
2. *After completing each chapter, write a summary of the chapter in your reading journal.*
3. *While reading, make connections with the text and write them in your reading journal.*
   a) *Text to Self – What does this remind me of in my life? What were my feelings when I read this?*
   b) *Text to Text – What does this remind me of in another book I've read? How is this different from other books I've read?*
   c) *Text to World – What does this remind me of in the real world? Have I heard about this before? (News, current events, school, etc.…)*

After Reading: Comprehension and Extension Activity

"After Reading" strategies provide an opportunity to summarize, question, reflect, discuss, and respond to text. After reading the book, work on the following questions with your child or students to check their level of reading comprehension and content mastery.
1. *Name three animals that wildlife biologists are studying in Yellowstone National Park. (Summarize)*
2. *Why do you think all the wolves disappeared in the lower 48 states? (Infer)*
3. *Why did the mountain pine beetle population increase in Yellowstone? (Asking Questions)*
4. *What would you study in Yellowstone and why? (Text to Self Connection)*

Extension Activity
Read about the 1980 eruption of Mount St. Helens. How would that eruption compare to an eruption from Yellowstone's supervolcano?

TABLE OF CONTENTS

INTRODUCTION

As pioneers explored the American West, there were rumors among fur trappers and other adventurers about a strange place high on a plateau. Some of these pioneers called it Yellowstone because of the yellow rock walls they saw.

Yellowstone's historical Grand Loop Road wraps throughout the major features in the park.

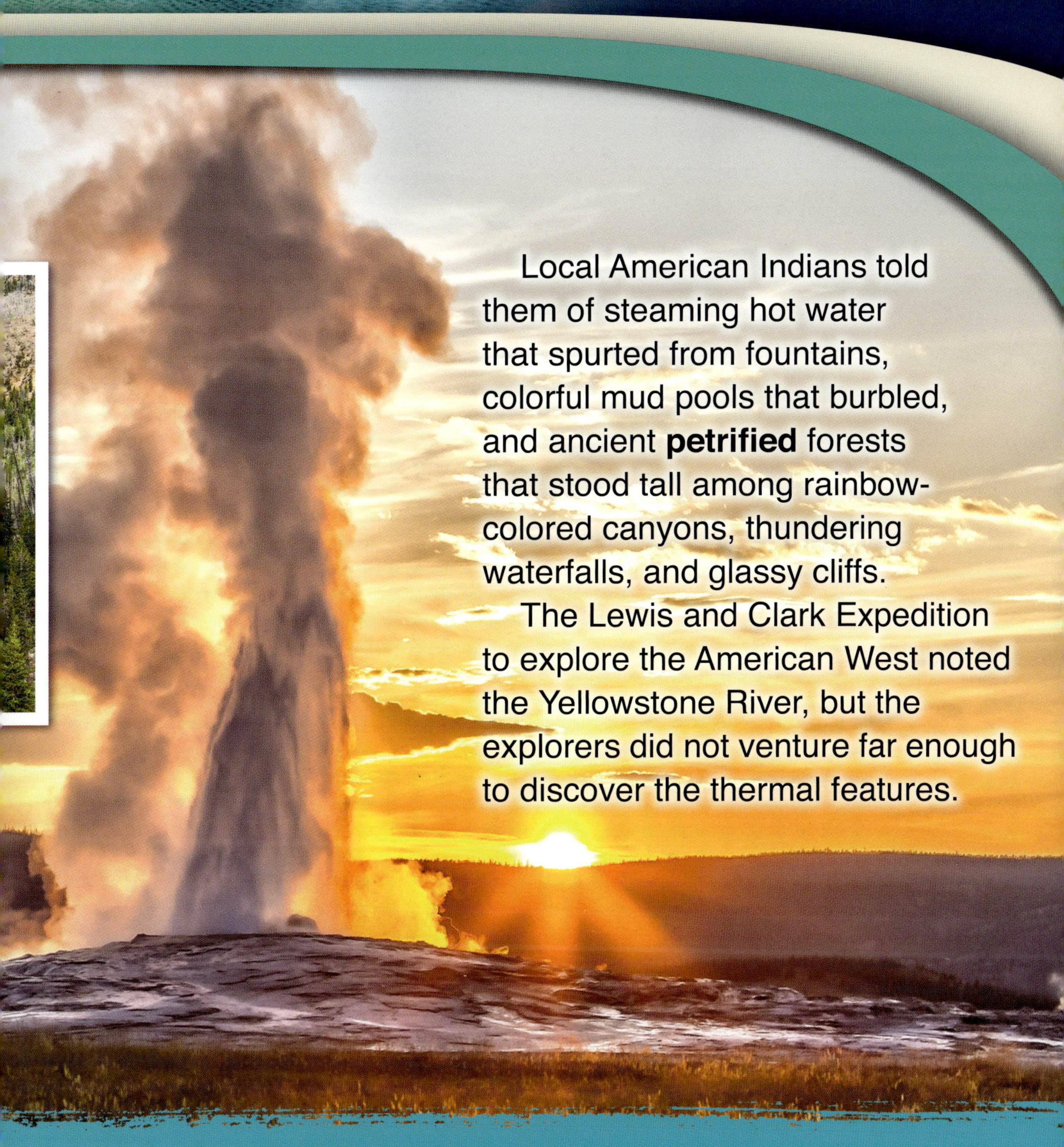

Local American Indians told them of steaming hot water that spurted from fountains, colorful mud pools that burbled, and ancient **petrified** forests that stood tall among rainbow-colored canyons, thundering waterfalls, and glassy cliffs.

The Lewis and Clark Expedition to explore the American West noted the Yellowstone River, but the explorers did not venture far enough to discover the thermal features.

Ancient Residents

Archeological evidence reveals that many American Indian tribes occupied or traveled through Yellowstone for more than 11,000 years, including ancestors of the Crow, Shoshone, Cayuse, Nez Percé, and other tribes.

The Yellowstone River follows the canyon formed after the Yellowstone Caldera eruption more than 640,000 years ago.

William Clark later created a map of Yellowstone using sketches and details from fur traders and others who traveled the wilderness. One fur trader was John Colter, who traveled with the Lewis and Clark expedition. He left the party and became a trapper. John is credited by many to be the first to discover what later became Yellowstone National Park.

Yellowstone became the United States' first national park in 1872. It became a popular destination for geologists and other curious scientists and explorers. They mapped the area and its many features. They described thousands of plants and animals that thrived there.

Modern researchers from around the world study a range of subjects, including earthquakes, hot springs, volcanoes, wolves, bison, and climate science.

Scientists measure the temperature and pH levels in Yellowstone's hot springs to study how organisms grow.

The First Scientists to Explore

Though many explorers visited and described different areas of Yellowstone, the first formal scientific expedition was the 1871 Hayden Expedition. The team consisted of a variety of scientists as well as artists and a photographer. It was the first time the world finally had visual proof that the mysterious place called Yellowstone existed.

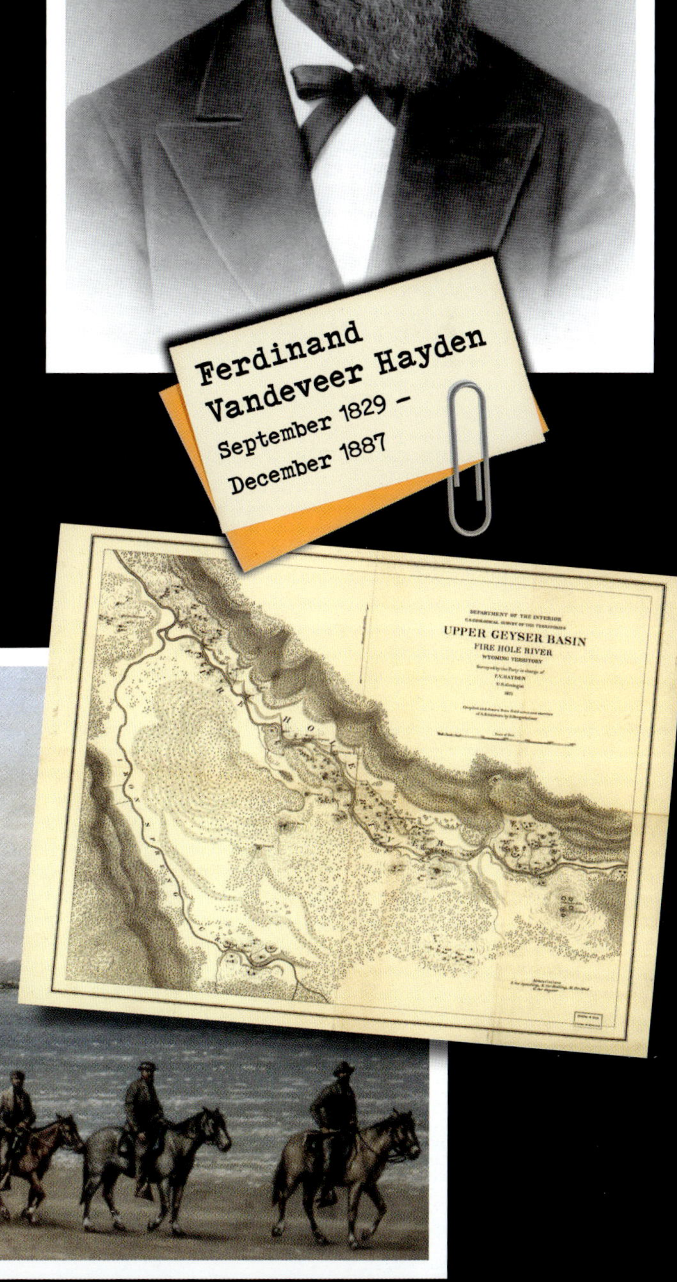

The 1871 Hayden Geological Survey passing by Yellowstone Lake; painting by William Henry Jackson

CHAPTER TWO

WILDLIFE RESEARCHERS

As the West was settled and developed, native wildlife found a last **refuge** in Yellowstone National Park. The Yellowstone Center for Resources (YCR) was set up in 1993 to bring together all of the park's science and resource management activities. The organization works to conserve and restore native species and their natural ecosystem.

A worker prepares a bison innoculation.

Mass Slaughter

Thirty to 60 million American bison were nearly hunted to extinction during the 1800s. It wasn't until killing wildlife inside Yellowstone National Park became illegal that the last few hundred animals were able to survive.

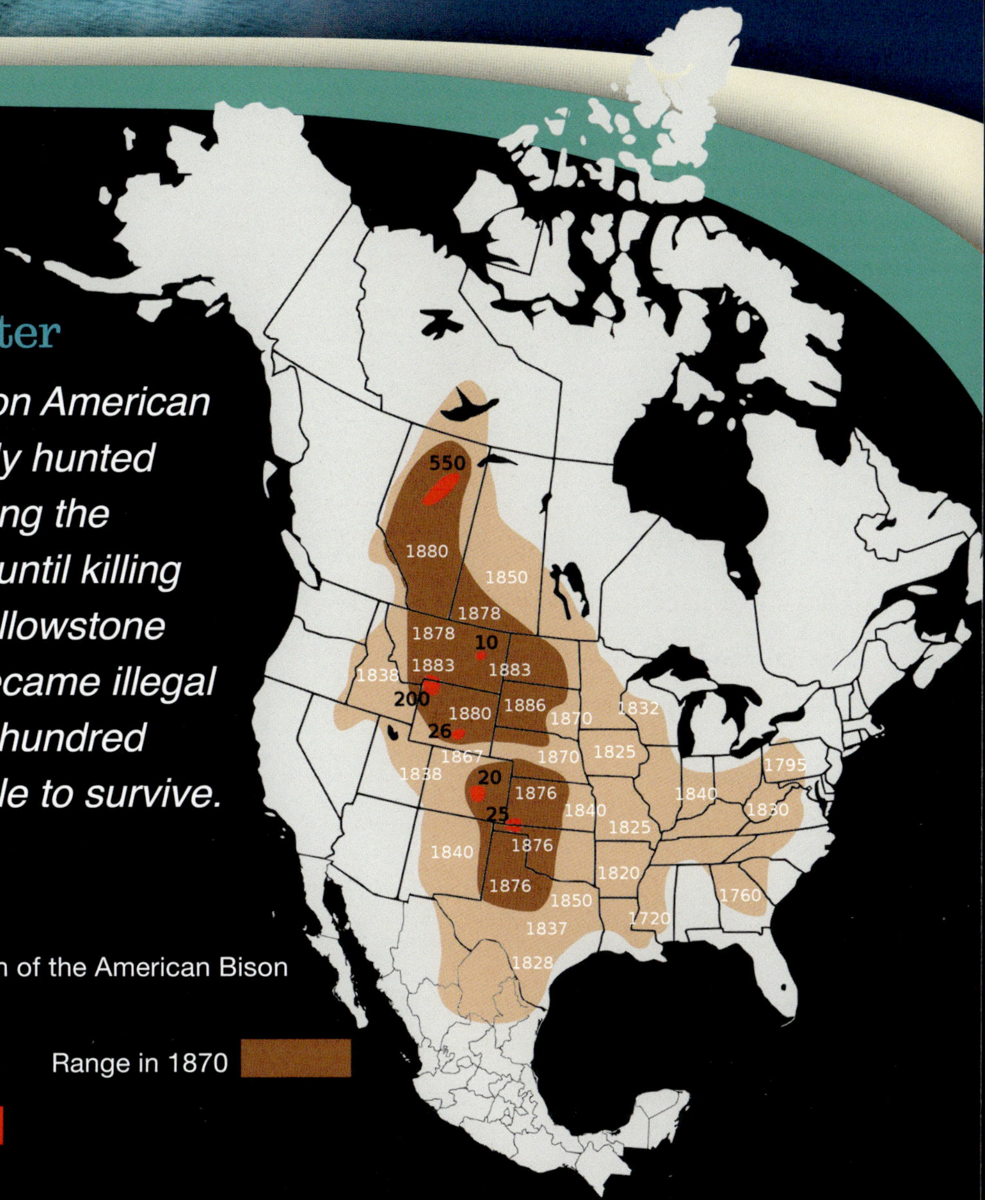

Map of the extermination of the American Bison to 1889

Original range

Range in 1870

Range in 1889

Bison bones from the 1870s were used for things like refining sugar, fertilizer, and making fine bone china.

The American bison that reside at Yellowstone National Park are some of the last wild, purebred bison. Unfortunately, they can carry a disease called brucellosis. Ranchers who graze cattle outside the park worry the disease will spread to their livestock if the bison leave the park boundaries.

Because of this concern, bison are often killed to control the population. This causes concern among wildlife biologists, who worry about the bison's **genetic** diversity. They suggest conservation efforts that would provide a more natural environment for the bison.

Some even hope to integrate bison in areas outside the park as a way to recover this nearly extinct native of North America.

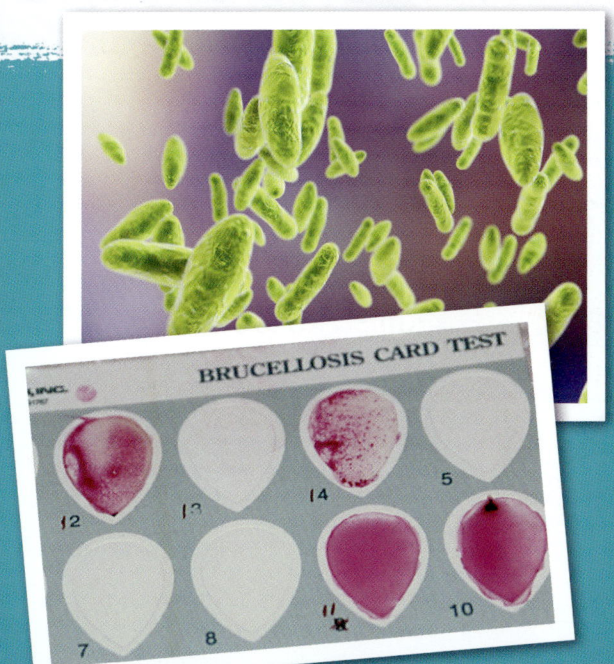

Imported Bacteria

Brucellosis is a bacterial disease that can harm pregnant cattle. Domestic cattle introduced from Europe in the late 1700s brought brucellosis to the native elk and bison of North America.

(Left) A brucellosis test card. Speckled results indicate a positive reaction for brucella antibodies; smooth pink indicates a negative reaction.

Gray wolves were once the main predator of elk, but by the mid-1900s, wolves had all but disappeared from their **historic** range in the United States, including inside Yellowstone National Park.

As a result, elk changed their habits, and their populations soared. They over-browsed young willow trees and many other plants, contributing to the loss of native vegetation and related wildlife species. This loss included beavers that needed willows to survive in winter.

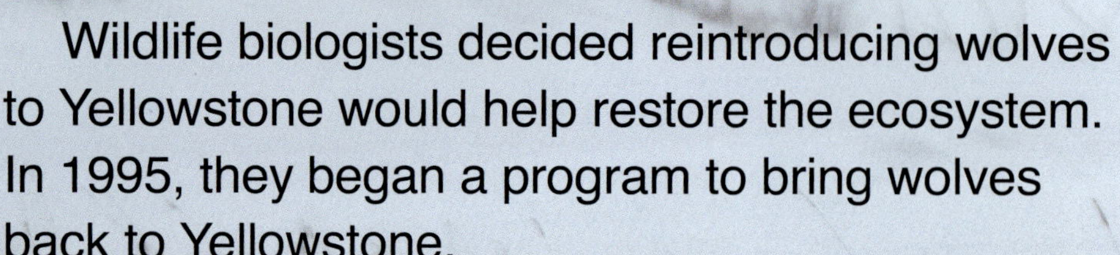

Wildlife biologists decided reintroducing wolves to Yellowstone would help restore the ecosystem. In 1995, they began a program to bring wolves back to Yellowstone.

After being housed and fed in temporary pens for a few weeks to get them used to the area and the food, the wolves were radio-collared and released.

Wildlife biologists carry a wolf in a crate.

wolves in Crystal Bench pen

Reprieve

*When the gray wolf was listed as an endangered species in 1974, the Endangered Species Act of 1973 required that their populations must be restored. It took 22 years for Yellowstone's **restoration** project to get underway.*

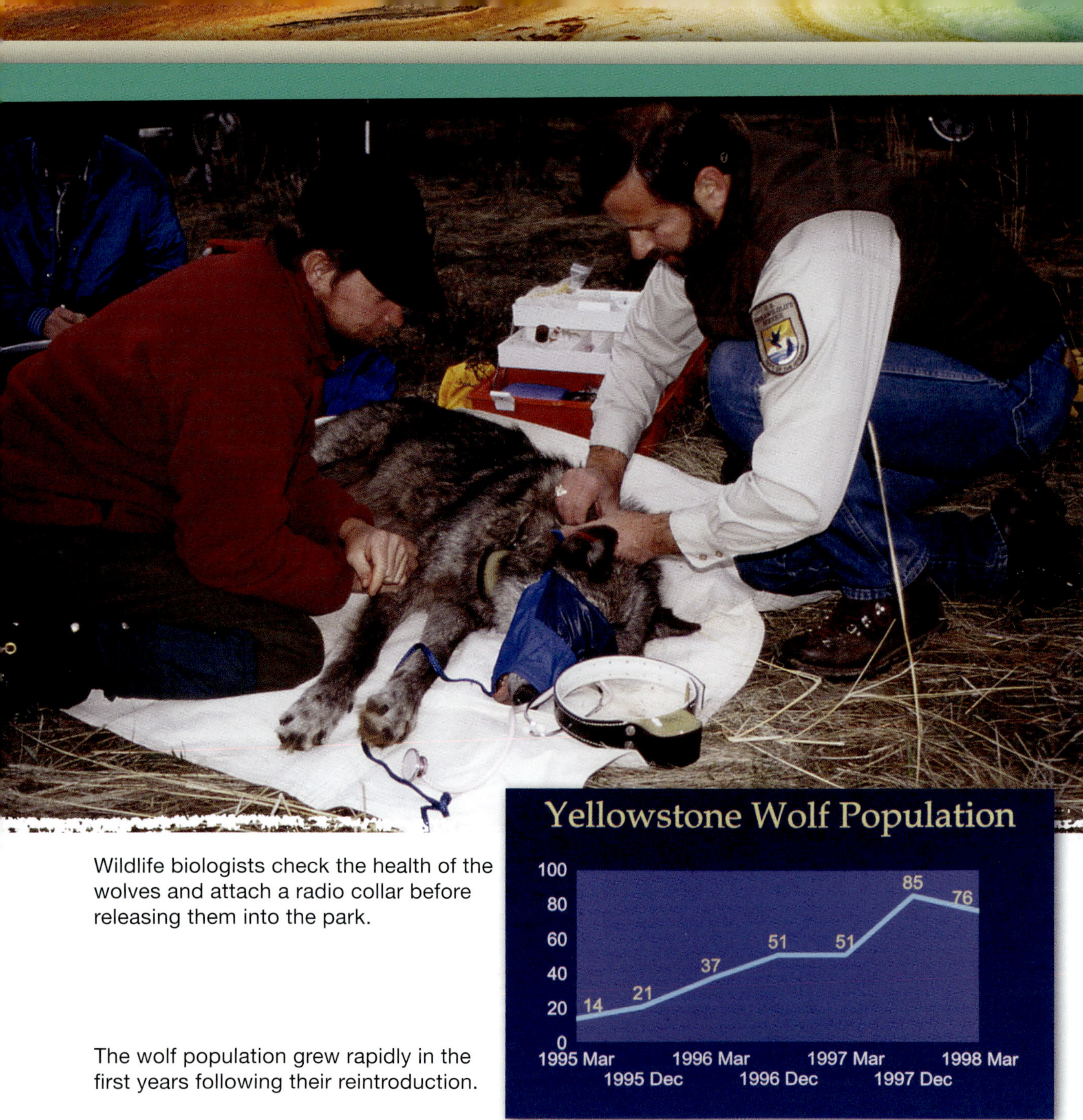

Wildlife biologists check the health of the wolves and attach a radio collar before releasing them into the park.

The wolf population grew rapidly in the first years following their reintroduction.

Scientists in Yellowstone are now studying the impacts of the wolf restoration project. Elk move around more because of the predators, and willows and other native trees and shrubs are growing again.

Beavers came back, constructing new dams and ponds, which restored water systems and fish habitat.

Wolves live and travel in packs, working together when hunting.

The willow stands provided homes for songbirds. In this restored living lab, biologists are able to see what happens when an ecosystem becomes whole again.

"It is like kicking a pebble down a mountain slope where conditions were just right that a falling pebble could trigger an avalanche of change." — Doug Smith, wildlife biologist for the Yellowstone Wolf Project

About 150 grizzly bears range in the Yellowstone National Park. As of 2016, there were about 700 in the Greater Yellowstone Ecosystem.

The Interagency Grizzly Bear Study Team (IGBST) is part of the 2016 Yellowstone Grizzly Bear Conservation Strategy. The goal is to help wildlife managers in their ongoing efforts to support the conservation of Yellowstone's grizzly bears.

A Small Range

Yellowstone and northwest Montana are the only places south of Canada where grizzly bears live. They are listed as a threatened species due to human-caused death as well as habitat loss.

IGBST researchers conduct a field study of a grizzly bear, tranquilizing and blindfolding it to prevent eye damage. They also provide oxygen to the bear while they collect biological data.

Biologists with IGBST and the National Park Service fit a grizzly bear with a radio collar.

Biologists trap, collect samples, and tag bears with tracking collars to monitor their health and numbers. Team members fly overhead to locate, observe, and track the bears in the Yellowstone region.

The radio collar sends signals to a tracking instrument that follows the bear's movements.

Wildlife biologist Mark Haroldson, along with a team of scientists and biologists, observe female bears with cubs. They also record **mortality** rates among the grizzlies. The information they gather helps to estimate the size of the bear population.

Recently, the research team monitored cone production in whitebark pine trees. The nutritious cones were an important part of a grizzly bear's pre-hibernation diet.

whitebark cone and seeds

The team noted that whitebark pine trees were dying due to mountain pine beetle damage. The beetle populations had increased because of warmer winters.

By studying a number of collared bears, the researchers noted that grizzly bears were adapting to the lack of this high-calorie food by shifting their diets to other foods, primarily meat. Grizzly bears are considered to be generalists, which means they can respond well to changes in their environment.

pine beetle

Biologists can determine a bear's diet by studying its scat.

Live-traps are used to capture bears for both study and relocation.

White settlement around Yellowstone contributed to the decline of native Yellowstone cutthroat trout, an important food source for bears, otters, mink, and several kinds of birds.

But the introduction of non-native fish, primarily lake trout and brook trout, hurt the cutthroat trout. Biologists watched the cutthroat spawning numbers in a Yellowstone Lake tributary plummet from more than 70,000 to about 500 in less than 30 years.

cutthroat trout

Their serious decline was mostly due to the non-native fish, which competed for food and preyed on the native fish.

Aquaculture

In the early 1800s, fish hatcheries were created to raise fish to stock the lakes, rivers, and streams in the U.S. Railroad carloads of non-native fish were transported across the west and released in the waterways, including the Yellowstone River.

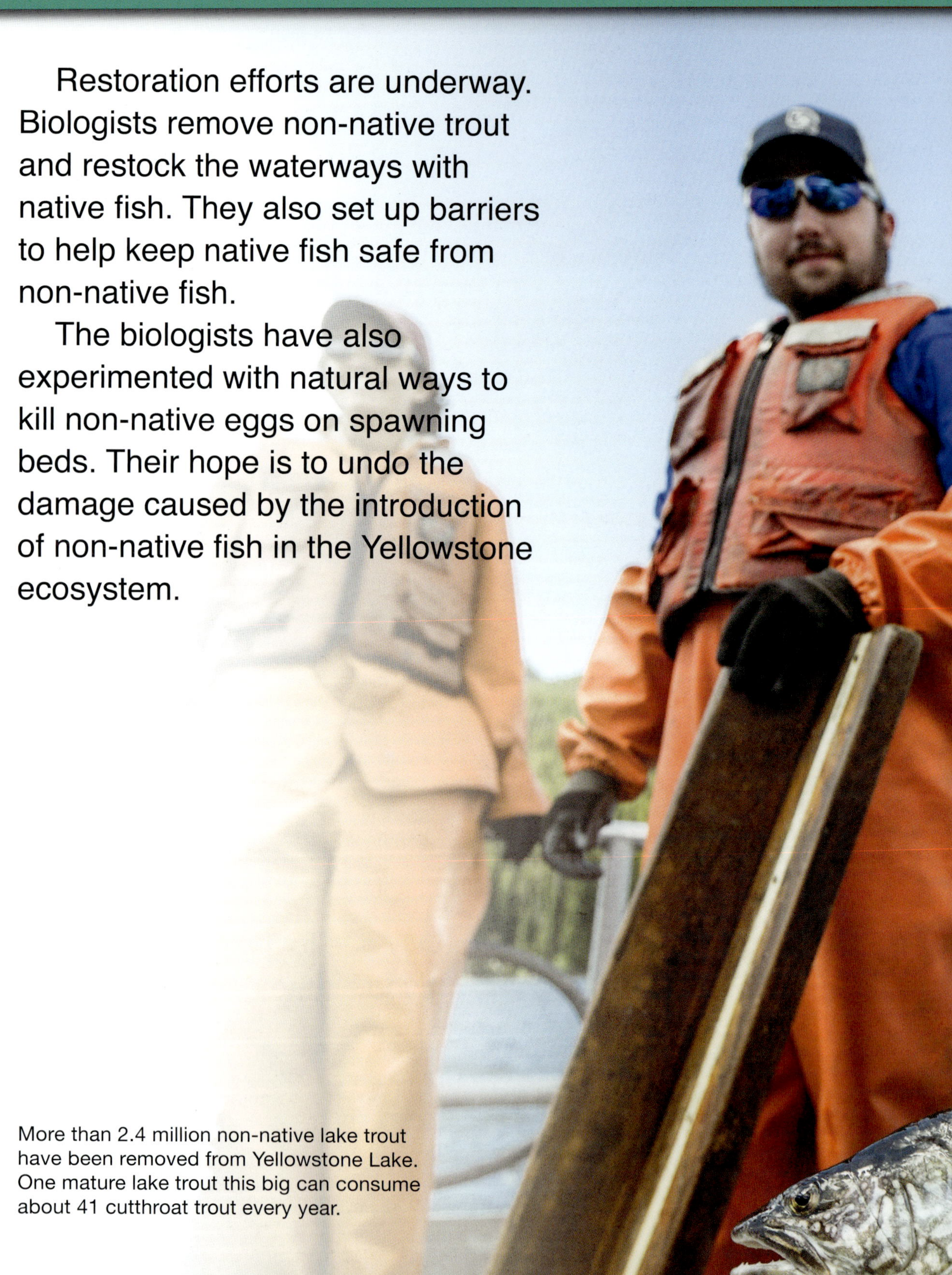

Restoration efforts are underway. Biologists remove non-native trout and restock the waterways with native fish. They also set up barriers to help keep native fish safe from non-native fish.

The biologists have also experimented with natural ways to kill non-native eggs on spawning beds. Their hope is to undo the damage caused by the introduction of non-native fish in the Yellowstone ecosystem.

More than 2.4 million non-native lake trout have been removed from Yellowstone Lake. One mature lake trout this big can consume about 41 cutthroat trout every year.

CHAPTER THREE

VOLCANOES AND EARTHQUAKES

About 600,000 years ago, a shallow sea covered Yellowstone. But a volcano erupted and covered the entire area in thick ash and lava. The mouth of the volcano collapsed and formed one of the largest **calderas** in the world.

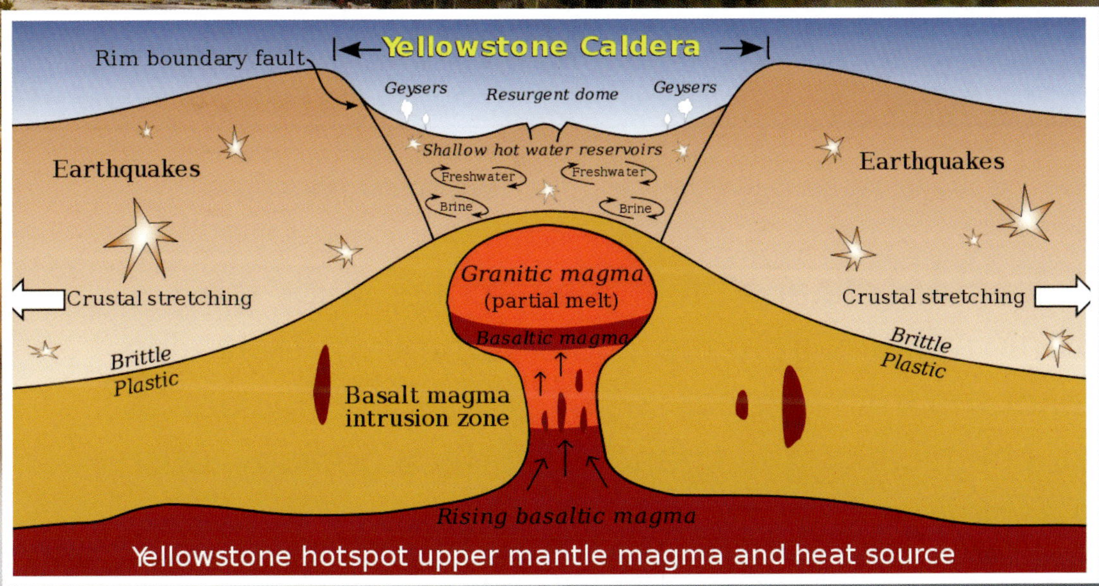

A shallow body of hot magma rock below the Yellowstone Caldera heats the dense salty water in cracks in the rocks above. When fresh water is introduced, it also becomes superheated.

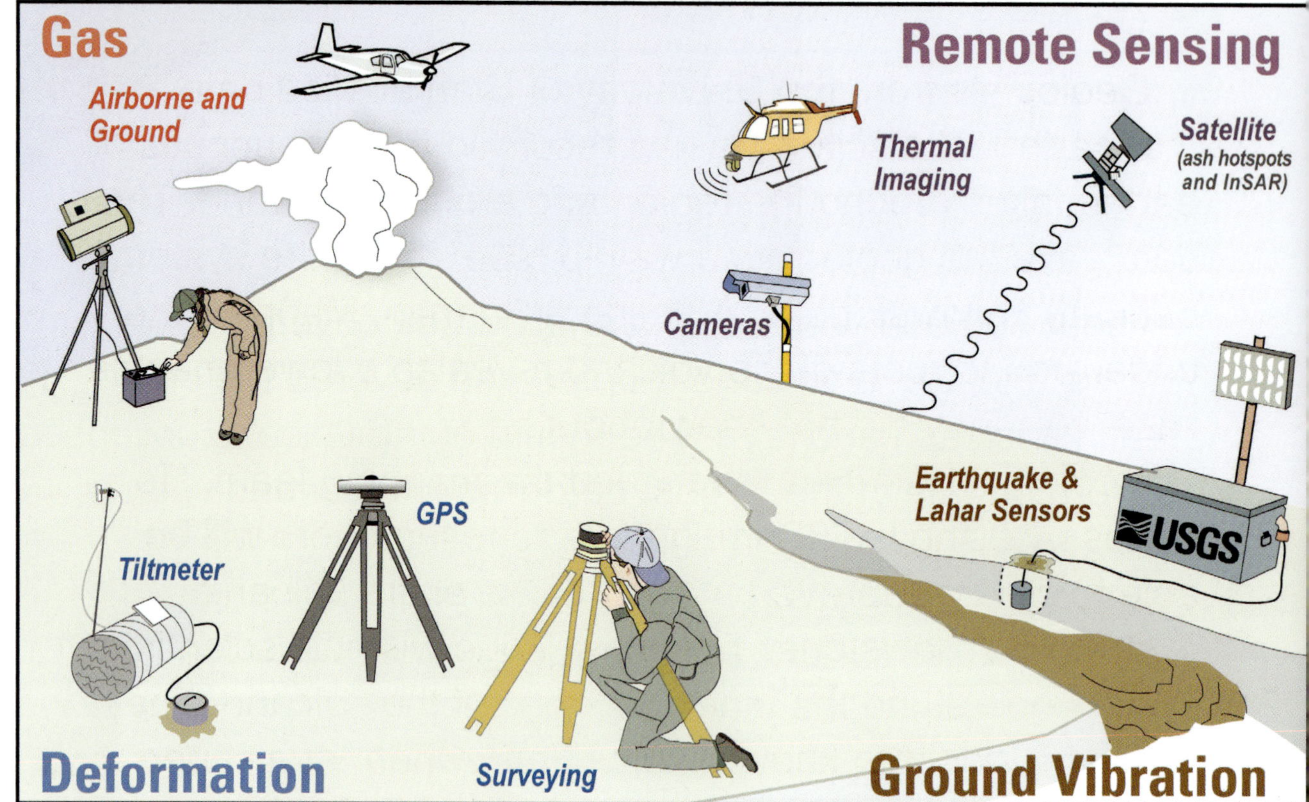

Geologists, earthquake scientists, and volcanologists use a wide variety of instruments to observe and monitor the geologic activity and chemistry around Yellowstone.

Volcanologists and other researchers study the volcanic remains from the ancient eruption. They also monitor the many processes of the caldera, including heat, chemical or gas changes, surface geology, uplift, and seismic activity.

Future Blast

Yellowstone's active super-volcano has the potential to produce an eruption 1,000 times stronger than the 1980 eruption of Mount St. Helens. It could have a serious effect on the global climate and ecosystem. The questions are, will it erupt again? And if so, when?

Geologists from the University of Utah applied data that earthquake scientists had recorded from thousands of earthquakes around the region and around the world. This data gave the geologists a way to "see" the entire system beneath Yellowstone by creating a 3D map. Mapping the underground roots of the volcano revealed a lower magma **reservoir** they did not know about.

Geologist Hsin-Hua Huang led the mapping team. He hopes by using his 3D image, future researchers will be able to create improved models of the entire volcanic system at Yellowstone. This knowledge will help scientists better understand the inner workings of the volcano. They would be closer to knowing the "if and when" of a super-volcanic eruption at Yellowstone National Park.

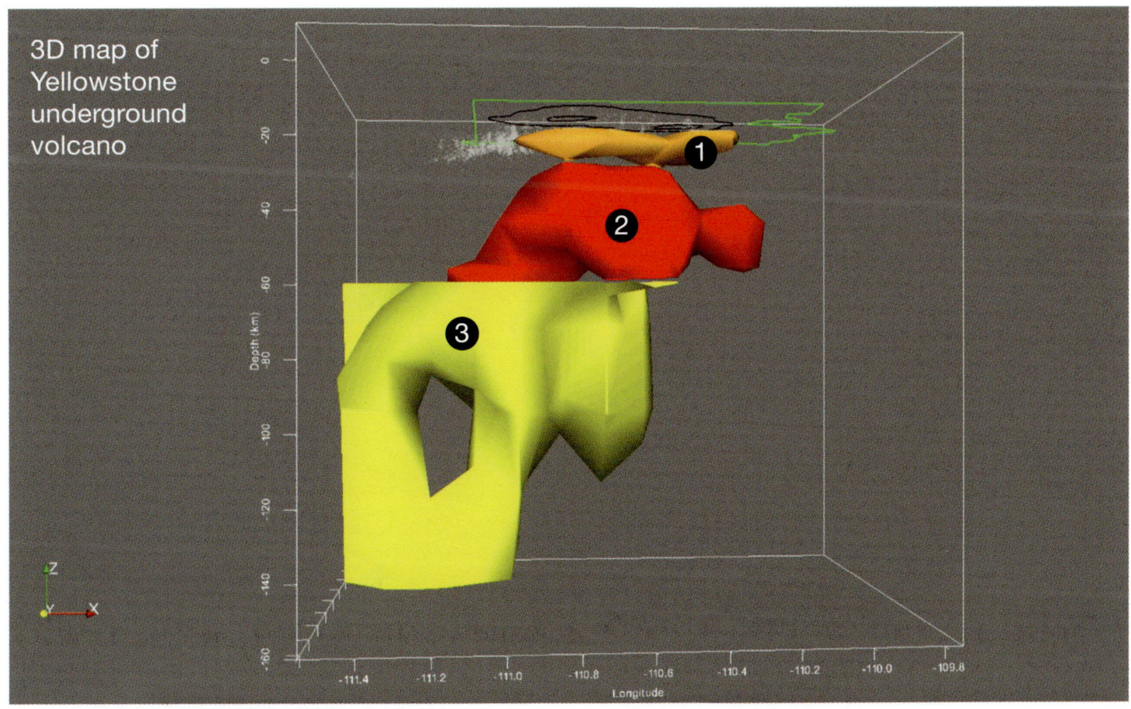

1. upper crustal magma chamber
2. lower crustal magma reservoir
3. mantle plume

CHAPTER FOUR

GEYSERS AND EXTREMOPHILES

There are more than 10,000 hydrothermal features in Yellowstone, including more than 300 geysers. A geyser only forms if there are hot rocks below, a **fissure** that water can spout through, a source of groundwater, and a reservoir of underground water. The active volcano fuels the geyser field at Yellowstone National Park. The field is about 50 miles (80 kilometers) wide.

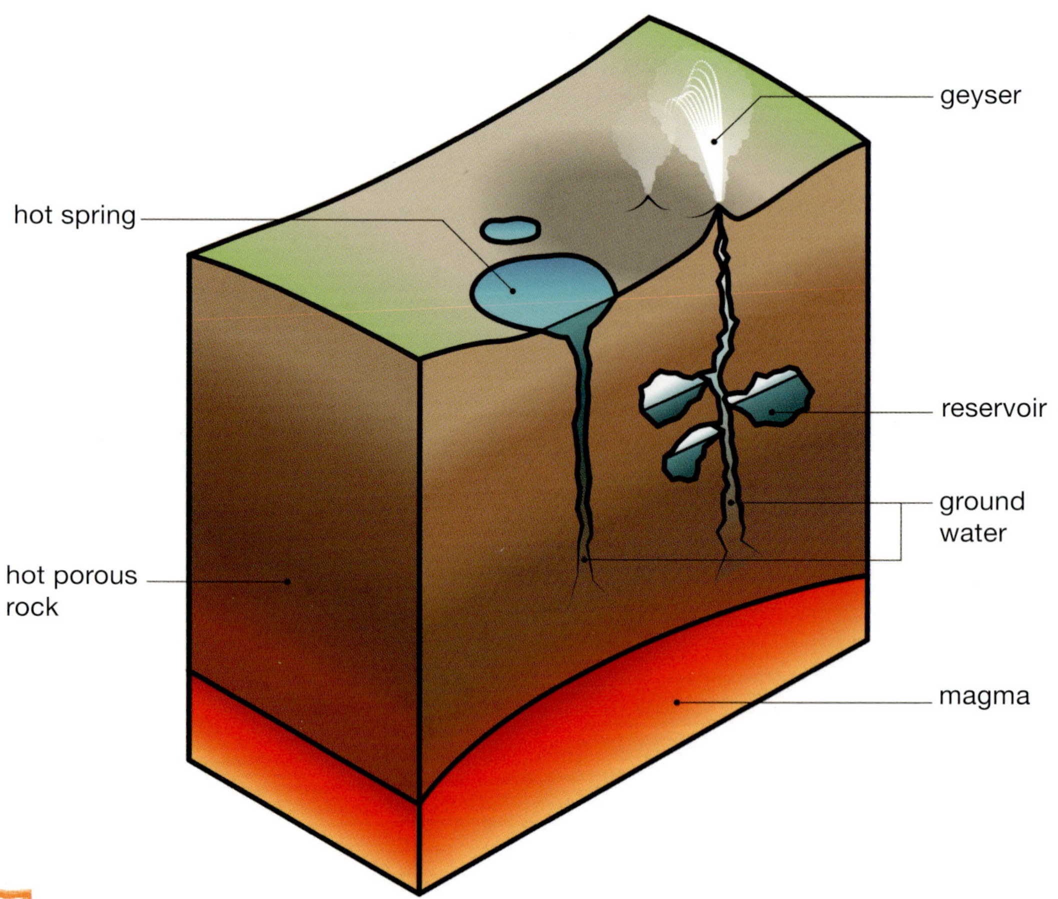

A thermal imaging camera uses infrared light to form a detailed temperature pattern, called a thermogram.

Volcanologists use thermal-imaging equipment to monitor temperatures across the geyser field. **Seismographs** are also set up to monitor seismic activity.

Collecting and analyzing water samples and measuring the amounts of certain gases gives scientists clues about changes in the magma system of the Yellowstone volcano.

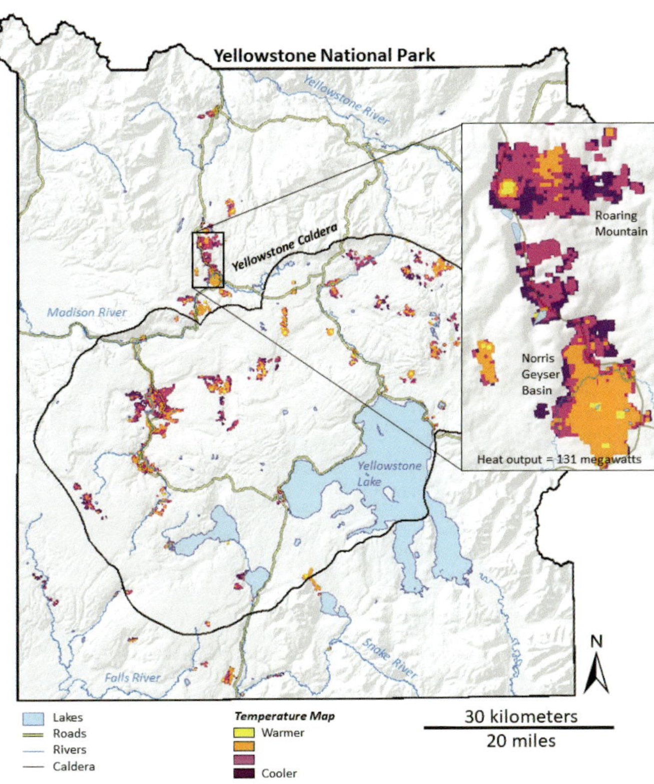

Temperature mapping of Yellowstone can also employ satellite thermal infrared images.

"We see gas emissions. We see all kinds of thermal activity. That's what Yellowstone does. That's what it's supposed to do. It's one of the most dynamic places on Earth." — Mike Poland, scientist in charge of the Yellowstone Volcano Observatory

Old Faithful has been erupting faithfully every 45 to 125 minutes for as long as anyone knows. The boiling hot water rises 106 to184 feet (32 to 56 meters) into the air. Scientists didn't know where the reservoir was that held the water, steam, and gas that fueled the famous geyser.

Scientists from the University of Utah along with geophysicist Robert Smith mapped Old Faithful's geology using a network of about 150 portable seismographs.

One model of a seismograph is a frame with a roll of paper bolted to the ground and a pen secured above it. When the ground shakes, the pen records the waveforms of the earthquake.

Old Faithful

Their seismic analysis provided details for a map of the underground plumbing system of the geyser. The map revealed the unknown reservoir of water that fed the geyser's surface vent. It also showed how the ground around the geyser vibrated between eruptions.

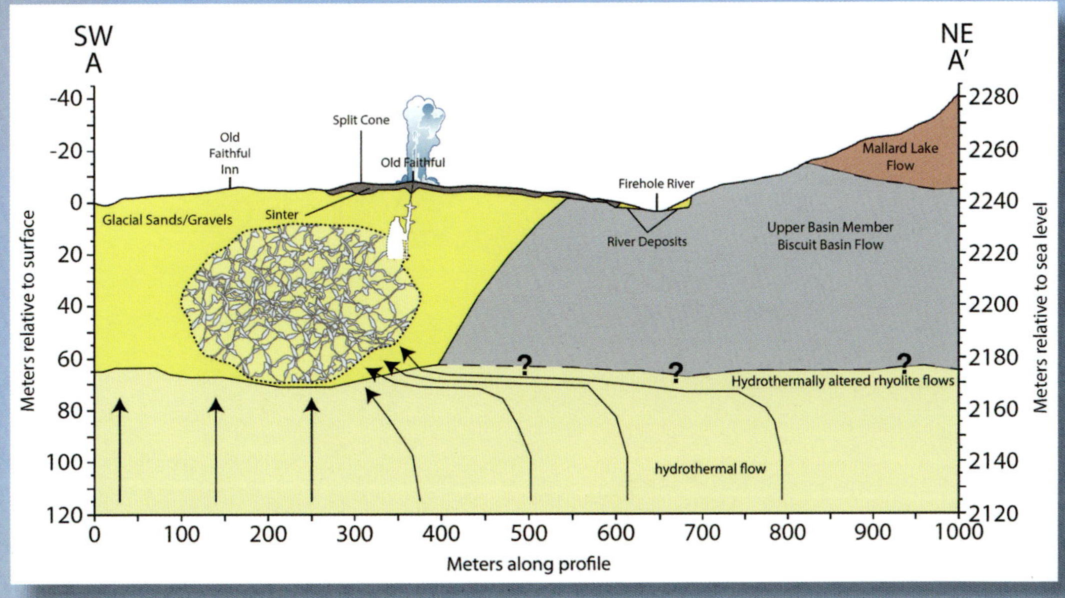

The new map of Old Faithful's plumbing system, shown here, is soon to be updated with even more details of the hidden underground structures.

"You fill a teakettle up with cold water and put it on the stove. And as the teakettle heats, it takes so many minutes. And then finally, when the pressure from the steam and hot water is big enough, it pops open the teakettle nozzle, if you wish, and out comes the steam." — Robert Smith, geophysicist

In addition to geysers, Yellowstone has colorful hot springs, blurping mud pots, steaming hot springs and gassy **fumaroles**. Microbiologists search for and study the unusual microbial life that thrives in the sizzling features in Yellowstone. One such life-form is **thermophilic** bacteria. Called an extremophile, these bacteria can survive exceptionally hot temperatures.

Grand Prismatic Spring

Red Spouter behaves like a mudpot in the spring and early summer. When the water table lowers in summer and fall, it turns into a hissing fumarole.

Extreme Heat Lover

In 1966, a researcher named Thomas Brock discovered a microorganism that could survive extreme heat and would kill most other living organisms. Microbiologists named these heat-loving creatures extremophiles.

The life forms found in the hydrothermal features in Yellowstone give scientists clues about Earth's ancient history and beginnings. Scientists continue to study the physical and chemical limits of how extremophiles live in such harsh environments.

Morning Glory Pool was once deep blue. Researchers discovered that pennies and other trash that humans tossed into the pool brought in new kinds of microbes, giving the pool its orange, green, and yellow colors.

Researchers also search the thermophilic communities for evidence of comparable life on other planets. Layers of rock found on Mars have features that are similar to rocks found in Yellowstone's hydrothermal features.

Burns Cliff, a layered rock wall on Mars, contains a mineral called jarosite. Jarosite, which only forms with acidic water, supports the kinds of extreme heat microbes that are found in Yellowstone.

Helpful Microbes

Extremophile research has helped scientists invent new kinds of possible commercial applications, including DNA research, new efficient production methods, and ways that food crops can survive high temperatures and drought.

CHAPTER FIVE

CLIMATE SCIENCE

Average temperatures in Yellowstone National Park are higher than they were 50 years ago, with warmer nights. The growing season has increased in some areas, and there are fewer days with snow on the ground compared to 50 years ago.

The warming temperatures are causing greater numbers of pest insects and plant diseases, as well as an increase in the number of large wildfires.

Biologists monitor whitebark pine trees in Yellowstone National Park for pine beetles and white pine blister rust, which was spread by a non-native fungus.

Yellowstone workers spray invasive non-native plants that affect the frequency of wildfires and impact native wildlife populations.

The variety of field studies happening in Yellowstone helps scientists better understand how ecosystems are reacting to climate change. Park scientists collect data about plants, animals, and environmental conditions. These are all the vital signs that reveal the health of the park. The information helps park managers develop a climate change response and monitoring plan.

Yellowstone's wetlands are already drying up, which affects species such as boreal chorus frogs, beavers, and trumpeter swans. The loss of plant life in the wetlands has harmful effects on water storage and natural firebreaks.

There are more than 357 square miles (924 square kilometers) of wetlands in Yellowstone, which includes marshes, wet meadows, and hydrothermal pools.

boreal chorus frogs

trumpeter swans

High elevations will possibly feel the greatest impact of warming. The alpine plants and animals must adapt, move to higher ground, or perish.

pika

The Plight of the Pika

The American pika is an example of an alpine animal being affected by global warming. It is sensitive to temperature and has started to disappear throughout its historic range in Yellowstone.

Yellowstone National park is a prime example of how climate change can affect natural resources. Armed with the scientific data, management teams are working to incorporate more climate-friendly park practices. At Yellowstone, renewable energy is replacing the use of fossil fuel energy.

Biodegradable products are replacing non-sustainable products. Buildings are being updated to be more energy efficient. Updated water systems are reducing water consumption. Treated wooden walkways are being replaced with recycled plastic wood products.

Yellowstone has been replacing asphalt roads with paving material made from recycled tires. The improved road system will help reduce erosion and runoff.

"In the future, national parks may tell the story of our collective success in dealing with climate change, moving to a way of life in greater harmony with the natural processes that operate on our planet. After all, Earth is the only planet we can call home."
— National Park Service, U.S. Department of the Interior

MAP THE INVASIVE WEEDS

Non-native plants can have a negative impact on the native population. It is a global problem, not just in Yellowstone National Park. Seek out the invasive plants in your yard, park, or school and map them for future monitoring or removal.

Supplies

- tape measure
- notebook and pen or writing tablet
- resource books
- flagged area for your study

Directions:

1. Use the resource books to identify the native and invasive plant species in your flagged area.

2. Draw a line down the middle of a page in your notebook. Walk the area and write down the native and the invasive plants you see, with native in one column, and invasive in the other. Sketch pictures of the leaf, seeds, and flowers, if present.

3. Measure from the perimeter to the plant from two directions and map the location of the plant. If there is a group, roughly circle the general location within your flagged area.

4. Write the results of your findings in a report.

Glossary

calderas (kawl-DARE-uhs): large volcanic craters

fissure (FIZ-jur): a narrow opening, especially one caused by splitting

fumaroles (FOO-muh-rols): holes in a volcanic region that release hot gases and vapors

genetic (juh-NET-ik): the way personal characteristics are passed from one generation to another through genes

historic (hiss-TOR-ik): an event that was important in the past or will be seen as important in the future

mortality (mor-TAL-uh-tee): the state of being unable to live forever

petrified (PET-ruh-fide): turned to stone because of minerals that seeped in

refuge (REF-yooj): a place that provides protection or shelter from danger or trouble

reservoir (REZ-ur-vor): a natural or artificial holding area for storing a large amount of water

restoration (rest-or-RAY-shuhn): the act of bringing something back to its original condition

seismographs (SIZE-muh-grafs): instruments used to measure and record the strength of earthquakes

thermophilic (thur-muh-FIL-ik): of, relating to, or being an organism living at a high temperature

Index

Show What You Know

1. What do microbiologists look for in Yellowstone National Park?

2. What do wildlife biologists study in Yellowstone?

3. What do volcanologists do in Yellowstone?

4. How do researchers monitor the location and population of grizzly bears in Yellowstone?

5. Name three instances where people have changed a policy at Yellowstone because of scientific research.

Further Reading

Jazynka, Kitson, *Wolf Rescue: All About Wolves and How to Save Them,* National Geographic Children's Books, 2014.

Koontz, Robin, *Volcanologists (Scientists in the Field),* Rourke Educational Media, 2015.

Siber, Kate, *National Parks of the USA,* Wide Eyed Editions, 2018.

About the Author

Robin Koontz is a freelance author/illustrator of a wide variety of nonfiction and fiction books, educational blogs, and magazine articles for children and young adults. Her 2011 science title, *Leaps and Creeps: How Animals Move to Survive*, was an Animal Behavior Society Outstanding Children's Book Award Finalist. Raised in Maryland and Alabama, Robin now lives with her husband in the Coast Range of western Oregon where she especially enjoys observing the wildlife on her property. You can learn more on her blog: robinkoontz.wordpress.com.

PHOTO CREDITS: Cover: Biologist holding trout courtesy of NPS, background photo on cover, title page and contents page © By Filip Fuxa—Shutterstock.com, card with paper clip art © beths—Shutterstock.com; page 4-5 geyser © Susanne Pommer, page 4 inset photo © Kenneth Keifer; page 6-7 © Bill45; page 12-13 © David Osborn, page 13 inset © Kateryna Kon; page 14-15 elk © Peter Bowman, wolf © Agnieszka Bacal, beaver © Kris Wiktor; page 16-17 © Agnieszka Bacal; page 20 © Nagel Photography; page 24-25 © Kevin Cass; page 28-29 © CherylRamalho; page 32 illustration © Zern Liew; page 34-35 © Wisanu Boonrawd, page 34 inset © Andrea Danti; page 36-37 © Lane V. Erickson, page 36 inset © Tricia Daniel; page 38 © Bertl123; page 40-41 © windsketch; page 42 wetland photo © HTurner, page 43 pika © BlueBarronPhoto, frogs © Ghost Bear, swans © Nick Pecker; page 44 © AlexLMX, page 45 © Olya_way. All photos from Shutterstock.com except: page 8 courtesy of NPS; page 9 map courtesy of the Library of Congress; page 10 courtesy of NPS, page 11 map © Cephas https://creativecommons.org/licenses/by-sa/3.0/deed.en; page 13 brucellosis card, and inset photos page 16 and 17 and all images pages 18-19 courtesy of NPS; page 21 large photo and bottom inset photo, page 22 bottom inset photo courtesy of Suzanna Soileau USGS, inset photo top courtesy of IGBST / USGS; page 22 bear USGS John Way; page 23, page 26-27 and page 28 courtesy NPS; page 30 and 33 courtesy of USGS; page 31 © Hsin-Hua Huang/Academia Sinica; page 35 © Sin-Mei Wu Department of Geology and Geophysics, University of Utah; page 37 inset courtesy of NPS, page 37 bottom inset photo © Amateria1121 https://creativecommons.org/licenses/by-sa/3.0/deed.en; page 37 courtesy of NASA/JPL/Cornell; page 39 courtesy of NASA/JPL/Cornell; page 41 courts of NPS / Diane Renkin; page 42 © NPS/Pat Perrotti

Edited by: Keli Sipperley

Produced by Blue Door Education for Rourke Educational Media. Cover design and page layout by: Nicola Stratford

Yellowstone / Robin Koontz
 (Natural Laboratories: Scientists in National Parks)
 ISBN 978-1-64369-021-6 (hard cover)
 ISBN 978-1-64369-113-8 (soft cover)
 ISBN 978-1-64369-168-8 (e-Book)
Library of Congress Control Number: 2018955986

Printed in the United States of America, North Mankato, Minnesota